Author: Tammi J. Salzano

Designed and Illustrated by CREATIVE QUOTIENT - A Repro Enterprise

Copyright © 2006 Scholastic Inc.

Scholastic and Tangerine Press and associated
logos are trademarks of Scholastic Inc.

Published by Tangerine Press, an imprint of
Scholastic Inc., 557 Broadway; New York, NY
10012

Scholastic Australia
Gosford NSW

Scholastic New Zealand
Greenmount, Auckland

10 9 8 7 6 5 4 3 2 1

ISBN 0-439-88736-4
Printed and bound in China

Introduction

Ever since humans have been on Earth, they've wanted to know more about it. From the earliest explorers in the New World to the astronauts who blast off into space, people have been fascinated with discovering all there is to know about the universe. With the telescope in your kit, you can make your own discoveries of the universe! Included are three lenses that allow you to view objects at various distances. So whether you're gazing at the stars or studying an interesting tree, you can explore your universe in a whole new way. And who knows what kinds of exciting things you might discover. Happy viewing!

What You Get in Your Kit

Your telescope has three lenses that you can use, depending on what it is that you're observing. The 20x and 30x lenses are good for observing objects that are closer to ground level, such as trees and birds (although bird-watching takes LOTS of patience!). To see the stars, you'll need the 40x lens.

The "x" on the lens tells you how much bigger an object will look with that lens. The 20x lens makes an object look 20 times bigger than when viewed with the naked eye, the 30x lens thirty times bigger, and the 40x lens forty times bigger.

Setting Up Your Telescope

WARNING! NEVER look at the Sun with your telescope! This can cause serious damage to your eyes.

1. Pick a quiet observation spot.

2. Unfold the tripod so that the legs are extended as far as they can go.

3. On the underside of the telescope, you'll see a black knob with ridges. Unscrew the knob, and take it off the telescope. You now have a black screw sticking out of the telescope.

4. Hold the telescope firmly in one hand and thread the black screw into the hole at the top of the tripod. Put the black knob on the screw and turn to tighten.

5. Choose the lens you want to use and put it lens-side-up into the holder at the end of the telescope.

6. Adjust the focus by turning the two small black knobs near the lens.

7. When you're finished viewing, always be sure to disassemble your telescope to keep it safe.

Patience, Please!

It will take practice to get good at observing objects with your telescope. If you don't see much right away, don't give up! Try changing the lens or adjusting the focus. You might also need to move to an area that has more or less light, depending on what you're looking at. And remember that most great discoveries take time!

The Birth of the Telescope: Hey, That's My Idea!

Imagine inventing something totally cool. Now imagine watching someone else become famous for your invention. That's exactly what happened to a man from the Netherlands named Hans Lippershey. In 1608, Lippershey applied for a patent for the first telescope, but he didn't get it. A year later, Galileo Galilei developed his own telescope and was credited as the inventor because of his incredible discoveries.

With his telescope, Galileo discovered craters on the Moon, the rings around Saturn, and the moons that orbit Jupiter. But perhaps Galileo's most important contribution to science came in the early 1600s, when he discovered that the planets revolve around the Sun, not Earth, as everyone believed at the time. Talk about turning the world on its head!

17th-century telescope

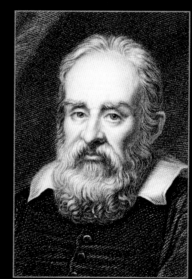

Galileo Galilei

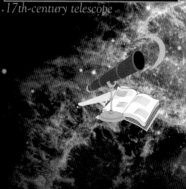

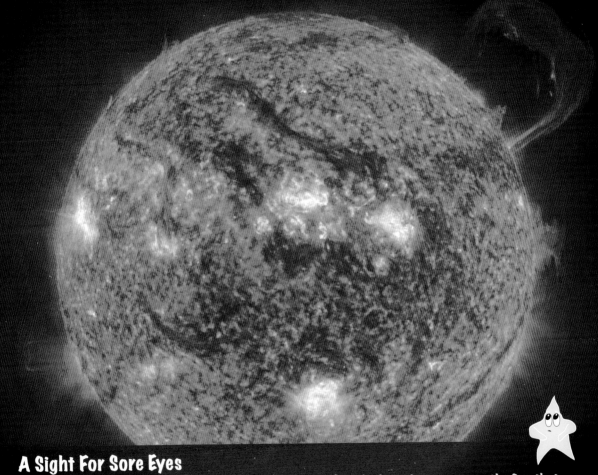

A Sight For Sore Eyes

Galileo was one of the first scientists to observe sunspots, which are large spots on the Sun that are cooler than the surrounding surface. But because he looked at the Sun using a telescope, he badly damaged his vision!

It's all a Little Fuzzy

With the invention of the telescope, scientists could view parts of our universe that they'd only dreamed of before. But there were limitations. In order to view objects in the sky, one had to look through the clouds, dust, and gases that are in the air around the earth. By the time the telescope focused on an object high in the sky, the image was blurry because of all of the material in the air.

What's a scientist to do? In 1940, the idea was born to have a telescope positioned up in space. The telescope could then send images of whatever it was looking at back to scientists on Earth. The images would be much sharper than those from telescopes on the ground. What an idea! But would it really work?

Got a Broom?

Earth's *atmosphere*—the mass of air surrounding the planet—is made up of layers of gases about 500 miles (805 km) thick. That's a lot of dust!

Presenting...The Hubble Telescope

In 1990, after years of planning and building, the National Aeronautics and Space Administration (NASA) completed one of the most well-known space telescopes, the Hubble telescope. Hubble was launched into orbit 380 miles (612 km) above Earth's surface, where it was to remain for about 20 years.

Named after American astronomer Edwin Hubble, the Hubble telescope had a big job. It would explore our entire solar system, sending images from space to scientists in labs here on Earth. From the data that Hubble sent, scientists would be able to learn all kinds of things about our world, including the age of the universe and how galaxies, planets, and stars were created.

No Batteries Required

The Hubble telescope is connected to computers on Earth so scientists can track its movements. But it's the Sun—and the large solar panels on the telescope—that supply Hubble with the energy to keep orbiting.

Hubble Fast Facts

Length: 43.5 feet (13.25 m) · Weight: 24,500 pounds (11,100 kg) · Cost to build: $1.5 billion U.S.

The Need for Speed

The size of a large school bus, the Hubble telescope orbits the earth at 5 miles per second (8 km/s). If cars were that fast, you could go from New York to California in only ten minutes!

In order to do its job, Hubble has to observe objects at large distances. It also needs to give images that are clear so that scientists can study them. The Hubble telescope is so accurate that if you were to copy how well it can focus on an object, you would need to shine a laser light steady on a dime that's 200 miles (322 km) away. Not exactly an easy task!

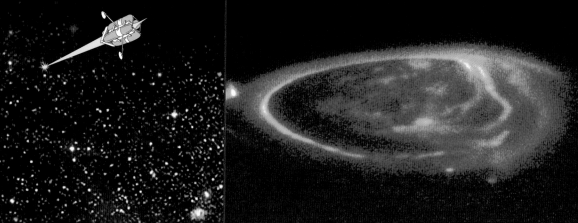

Hubble has taken some amazing pictures of our universe. But as important as Hubble has been to science, it was built to last for only about 20 years. Scientists retire old telescopes by crashing them into the ocean! Plans are already underway to replace Hubble, however. Scientists are currently planning the James Webb space telescope, which will be much bigger than Hubble and will provide images that are even clearer. It's scheduled to launch into orbit in 2013.

The World Beyond Earth

Okay, so you've got your cool new telescope, you've learned a couple of neat things about space, and you're ready to start viewing. But what should you look at? How about the sky!

Astronomy is the study of objects outside of Earth's atmosphere, such as the stars, planets, and other objects in space. Our solar system is part of the Milky Way **galaxy,** which is a group of stars, dust, and gas that's held together by gravity. Astronomers want to learn as much as possible about the world that exists beyond Earth. Space is such a large place that we're only

just beginning to understand what's out there. There's so much still to learn, so who knows—maybe you'll make an important discovery!

Stars of the Show

Stars are some of the most observed objects in the sky. On a clear night, there's no end to the stars that you can see. Many stars are part of **constellations,** which are groups of stars that form patterns.

Different constellations are visible each season of the year. The constellations you see also depend on where you live. If someone who lives north of the equator sees a constellation in the summer, a person south of the equator would see that same constellation in the winter.

The **equator** is an imaginary line around Earth that divides the planet into the northern and southern hemispheres.

Many constellations can be seen with the naked eye, but using your telescope will give you a better view. Here are some of the more famous constellations to look for:

The seasons listed are for the northern hemisphere.

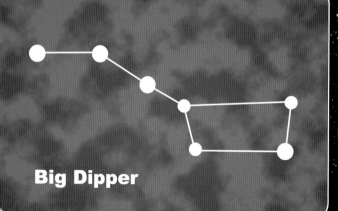

Big Dipper

Big Dipper (*all seasons*)

Star Light, Star Bright
One of the stars in the Big Dipper is Polaris, the North Star. Polaris is the brightest star in the night sky.

The Big Dipper and the Little Dipper are actually part of larger constellations. The Big Dipper is part of Ursa Major the Great Bear. The Little Dipper is part of Ursa Minor the Little Bear.

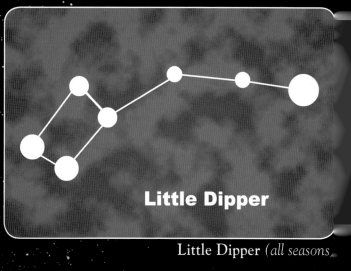

Little Dipper

Little Dipper *(all seasons)*

Orion

Orion the Hunter *(winter)*

Hunting for the Hunter
One easy way to find Orion is to look for the three stars that make up its belt.

Aries the Ram (*autumn, winter*)

Gemini the Twins (*winter*)

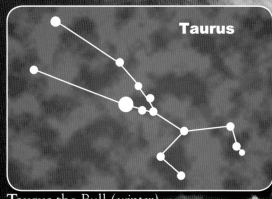

Taurus the Bull (*winter*)

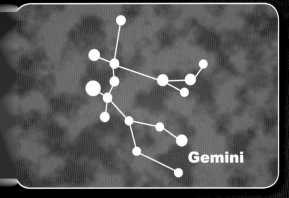

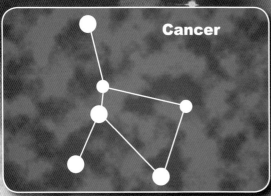

Cancer the Crab (*winter, spring*)

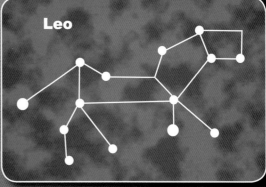

Leo the Lion (*spring*)

Starry, Starry Night
There are **88** constellations in the night sky.

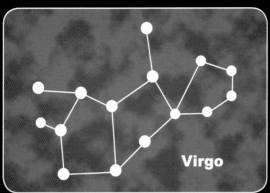

Virgo the Maiden *(spring)*

Scorpius the Scorpion *(summer)*

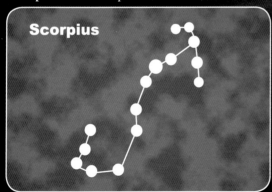

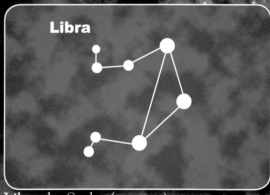

Libra the Scales *(summer)*

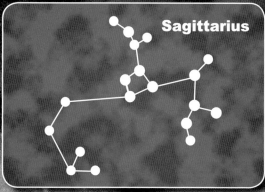

Sagittarius the Archer (*summer*)

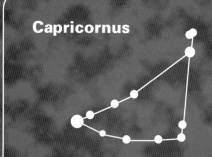

Capricornus the Goat (*autumn*)

It's all Greek (and Roman) to Me!
Many of the names of the constellations come from figures in Greek and Roman mythology.

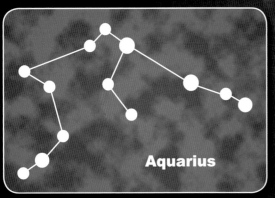

Aquarius the Water Carrier (*autumn*)

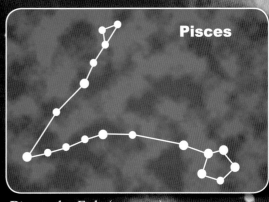

Pisces the Fish (*autumn*)

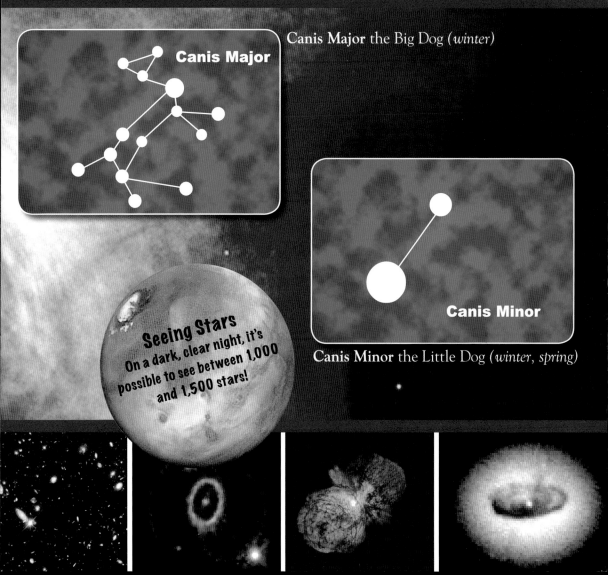

Canis Major the Big Dog *(winter)*

Canis Major

Canis Minor the Little Dog *(winter, spring)*

Canis Minor

Seeing Stars
On a dark, clear night, it's possible to see between 1,000 and 1,500 stars!

Next Stop: Planets!

Just like the constellations, most of the planets can be seen from Earth without a telescope. (But what fun is that, right?) The exceptions are Neptune and Pluto, which require a high-powered telescope because they're so far away. Also like the constellations, different planets are visible at different times of the year. As with any object in the sky, the stronger the telescope you're using, the more details you'll see.

All of the planets are either **terrestrial** or **jovian**. Terrestrial planets are made of rock and include Mercury, Venus, Earth, and Mars. The jovian planets, which are made of gases, are Jupiter, Saturn, Uranus, and Neptune. Pluto doesn't fit into either group, because it's made of ice and rock. In fact, many scientists don't think it should be called a planet at all!

Mercury is a bit of a mystery planet. It's rarely seen because the Sun's glare makes it hard for telescopes in space to take pictures of it. Temperatures on Mercury can go as high as 750 degrees F (400 degrees C) during the day and as low as minus 320 degrees F (minus 200 degrees C) at night. Imagine trying to decide what to wear in *that* kind of weather!

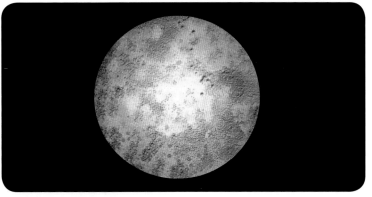

The planet **Venus** is about the same size as Earth. It's not possible to live on Venus, though, because the air isn't breathable. Besides, you'd have to like it really hot—the temperature hovers around 800 degrees F (430 degrees C)!

Earth is home to all known life in the universe. The temperatures on Earth and its plentiful water make it an ideal place for living things to survive. This photograph of Earth was taken from the Moon by the Apollo 11 astronauts in July 1969. Imagine what it must have been like for the astronauts to be looking at home!

Known as the Red Planet, **Mars** is the only planet whose surface can be seen clearly from Earth. **Rovers**—unmanned robotic space vehicles—have explored Mars and have found that there almost certainly was water on the planet at one time. And if there was water, chances are very good that there was life!

Jupiter is the largest planet in our solar system. As many as 1,266 Earths would fit inside it! The Great Red Spot on Jupiter—the dark oval shape—is a huge storm made up of gases that swirl around like the winds in a hurricane. But it's no ordinary storm—those gases move around at 225 mph (360 km/h)!

Saturn is the second largest planet at 74,500 miles (120,500 km) wide. The rings around Saturn—which are made of chunks of ice—make it one of the most recognizable planets. Some of the ice chunks in Saturn's rings are as big as a small car!

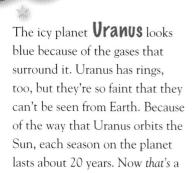

The icy planet **Uranus** looks blue because of the gases that surround it. Uranus has rings, too, but they're so faint that they can't be seen from Earth. Because of the way that Uranus orbits the Sun, each season on the planet lasts about 20 years. Now *that's* a summer vacation!

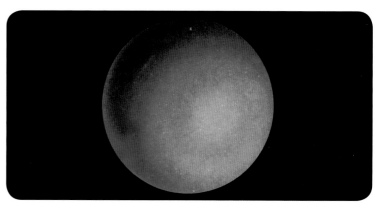

Neptune is similar to Uranus in that it, too, has rings that are not visible from Earth. Neptune used to have a storm like Jupiter called the Great Dark Spot, but the storm has since disappeared. You'd need to hold on to your hat on Neptune—the winds on the surface of the planet blow at 1,200 mph (2,000 km/h)!

The smallest of all the planets, **Pluto** is so far out in space that it takes five and a half hours for sunlight to reach it. It takes only eight minutes for sunlight to reach Earth! Scientists have not been able to capture a clear picture of Pluto, because it's so far away. In 2006, an unmanned rocket carrying a spacecraft was sent to explore Pluto. But this is more than just an overnight trip—it will take the rocket almost 10 years to reach Pluto!

Earth's **Moon** is one of the most studied objects in the night sky. It has lots of craters on it, caused by rocks and other space debris that crashed into it. The Moon is 230,400 miles (384,000 km) from Earth, and it's actually moving even away! Every year, the moon drifts about 1½ inches (3.8 cm) farther from us. To this day, 12 men have walked the surface of the Moon.

Here are some other sights that you might see in the night sky:

Meteors, or shooting stars, are formed when a piece of debris (such as rock) enters Earth's atmosphere. This causes the debris to glow and results in the light that we see streaking across the night sky. On any night, you can see between two and seven meteors, and they always appear brighter and faster after midnight. Keep your eyes focused on the sky—meteors can move very quickly!

Comet

Comets are a mixture of dust and frozen gases. The word *comet* comes from the Greek meaning long-haired, which describes a comet's tail. A comet is named for the person who discovers it. Two famous ones are Halley's Comet and the Hale-Bopp Comet. Halley's Comet is visible from Earth every 76 years, so it should make its next flyby in 2062.

Auroras are curtains of lights formed by gases in the atmosphere that glow when conditions are right. These beautiful lights are typically yellow-green, blue-violet, or red. Because the solar winds blow them around, they appear to bend in the sky.

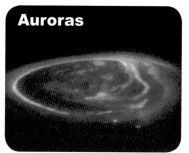

Auroras

Meteor

Night Lights
People north of the equator can see an aurora called the aurora borealis, or northern lights. South of the equator, you'll see the aurora australis, or southern lights.

Conclusion

Hopefully you've been able to observe some of the amazing objects in and around our world. If you want to learn more about stargazing, check with a local observatory, or find out if there's an astronomy group in your area. Some state and local parks also hold stargazing events, so check them out, too, and keep your eyes on the stars!

Reach for the... Ground?

You can use your telescope to explore your world at ground level, too! Drop in your 20x and 30x lenses and be on the lookout for interesting trees, flowers, animals, and even birds. Keep in mind that bird-watching takes lots of practice and patience. Our feathered friends are quick!

Glossary

astronomy: the study of objects outside of Earth's atmosphere, such as the stars, planets, and other objects in space

atmosphere: the mass of air surrounding a planet

constellations: groups of stars that form patterns

equator: an imaginary line around Earth that divides the planet into the northern and southern hemispheres

galaxy: a group of stars, dust, and gases held together by gravity

jovian: planets made of gases

rovers: unmanned robotic space vehicles

sunspots: large spots on the Sun that are cooler than the surrounding surface

terrestrial: planets made of rock